There's nobody else
J'd rather **lollygag** with!

To my wonderful Domi
on **29**th birthday ♡

Z.

sep 2021

✳✛✳✳ **THE** ✳✳✳✛✳

History
— OF —
Insults

Over 100 put-downs,
slights, and snubs
through the ages

Compiled by Nathan Joyce

Looks like a
barrel border
to me.

DOG 'n' BONE

That bacon-fed clodhopper looked like death's head on a mop stick; he'll be in an earth bath any day now.

TRANSLATION:
That greasy lout appeared unwell. He'll be in a grave soon, mark my words.

Published in 2017 by Dog 'n' Bone Books
An imprint of Ryland Peters & Small Ltd
20–21 Jockey's Fields   341 E 116th St
London WC1R 4BW   New York, NY 10029

www.rylandpeters.com

10 9 8 7 6 5 4 3 2 1

Text © Nathan Joyce 2017
Design and illustration © Dog 'n' Bone Books 2017

A CIP catalog record for this book is available from the Library of Congress and the British Library.

ISBN: 978 1 911026 30 3

Printed in China

Designer: Jerry Goldie

CONTENTS

INTRODUCTION

We know that the Ancient Greeks and Romans transformed the known world with their philosophy, culture, and technology, but it may be refreshing to learn that their pioneering innovations extended to insulting each other. It turns out that both Greek and Roman soldiers carved humorous messages into sling-shot balls before flinging them at their enemies. Some of the choice cuts include "Here's a sugar plum for you," "For Pompey's backside," and the timeless "Ouch!".

Shakespeare contributed to literature more than any writer before or after him. It may surprise you, however, to find out that this unparalleled genius enjoyed a well-placed "Your mamma" gag like the rest of us, kindly leaving one for us to uncover in *Titus Andronicus*. He was not the first, though. He was passing on a torch that had been lit in Ancient Babylonia (around 1,500 BCE) by

You, minion, are too saucy!

> *You lousy gongoozler!*

a cheeky student who alluded to an unknown mother's promiscuity. A significant moment in human civilization, for sure, but the "Your mamma" gag is trumped (I'm not even sorry— I'm contributing to a proud tradition) by an even more esteemed joke. That's right. Humanity's first contribution to written comedy was… a fart joke, dating back to 1,900 BCE. Alas, it wasn't I fart in your general direction, just for the record.

Since then, civilizations have come and gone, but

> *Go boil your shirt!*

their glorious insults remain, undimmed. In the pages that follow, you'll find some of the finest burns in history, courtesy of the Vikings, Medieval French, Song Dynasty Chinese, Victorians, and the Jazz Age Americans, among others. You'll also find a smattering of the most extraordinary, unusual put-downs from across the world, which are still proudly used today. I doff my cap to the Japanese.

CHAPTER 1

CLASSICAL CURSES

Abuse from the Romans,
Greeks, and Vikings.

> **You stink like a cheap latrine!**

TRANSLATION:
You absolutely reek!

TRANSLATION:
You are so insufferably dull that I may actually die of boredom!

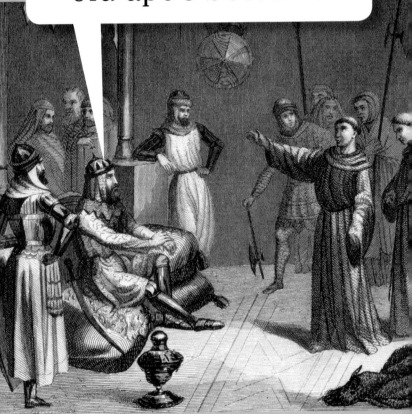

His painted cheeks are flabbier than an old ape's bottom!

TRANSLATION:
My word, his cheeks are as pale as they are chubby!

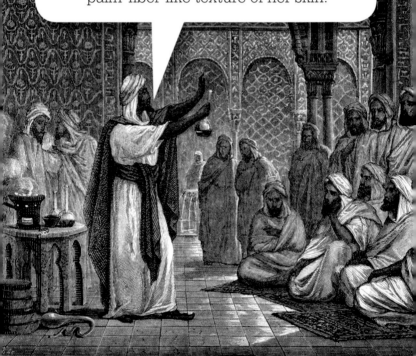

Her foul breath, the smell of fermented p**s which rose from her armpits and her groin, the putrid aura, like that of rotten garlic, which remained from the many times she had broken wind, her hairiness which was more than that of a hedgehog, and the palm-fiber-like texture of her skin.

TRANSLATION:
An unholy stink emanated from her as a result of her uncontrollable urination and sustained farting, on top of her considerable hairiness and prickly skin.

10

CHAPTER 2

BIBLICAL BANTER

Slander from the scriptures.

You son of a perverse and rebellious woman!

TRANSLATION:
You son of a b*h!**

TRANSLATION:
You faithless, short-sighted simpletons!

You snakes! You brood of vipers!

TRANSLATION:
You crafty, treacherous jerks!

As a dog returneth to his vomit, so a fool returns to his folly.

TRANSLATION:
Your idiocy seems to be a chronic condition.

16

My little finger is thicker than my father's loins.

I'm *ahem* a bigger man than my father.

Go and learn what this means!

You will need to acquire some more gray matter before you can understand what I'm saying, you cretins!

Nazareth! Can anything good come from there?

I support Bethlehem FC and I'm proud of it. Your town is a dump.

Baldy!

Hypocrites!

Dogs!

You can probably work these out for yourselves!

CHAPTER 3

MEDIEVAL MUD SLINGING

Norman French, Italian, and English invective.

You gluttonous evil-doer!

TRANSLATION:
You greedy, sinful monster!

You've eaten farro soup!

ROMEO und JULIA.
Nº 3. CAPULET stützt TYBALT, der von ROMEO verwundet.

LIEBIG COMPANY'S FLEISCH-EXTRACT.

Filthy worm head!

Thou woldest make me kisse thyn old breech, And swere it were a relyk of a saint, Though it were with thy fundement depeint! But by the croys which that seint Eleyne fond, I wolde I hadde thy coillons in myn hond, In stride of relikes or of seintuarie, Lat kutte hem of...

TRANSLATION:
You would force me to kiss your old trousers and swear they were relics of a saint, even though they had been stained by your arse! But by the cross which Saint Helen found, I wish that I had your balls in my hand instead of relics. Let's cut them off!

By God... thy drasty rhyming is not worth a turd!

TRANSLATION:
Do shut up you tiresome moron.

Do you yield, thou yaldson?

TRANSLATION:
Do you surrender, you son of a prostitute?

CHAPTER 4

TUDOR AND SHAKESPEAREAN INSULTS

Some 16th-century slights.

> *Get back here you pilgarlic, dull faitor!*

TRANSLATION:
Come here you bald, fat traitor!

You have taken my wife as your leman you rabbit-sucker. A pox upon you!

But I saw you with a laced-mutton yesterday— I thought you were a wittol!

Who are you calling fustilugs, you mooncalf!

Thou art as loathsome as a toad.

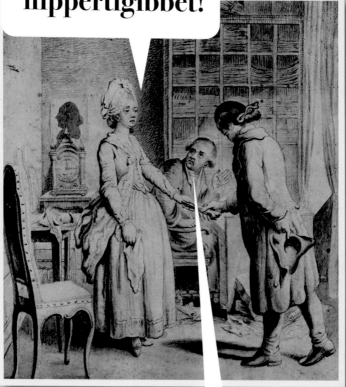

And he had the gall to call me a gorbellied flippertigibbet!

TRANSLATION:
He had the nerve to call me a fat gossip-monger!

What a deboshed swinge-buckler!

TRANSLATION:
What a drunken bully!

You, minion, are too saucy!

TRANSLATION: You, hussy, are too insolent!

Thy tongue outvenoms all the worms of the Nile.

TRANSLATION: Your breath is appalling.

Methink'st thou art a general offence and every man should beat thee.

TRANSLATION: You are universally irritating and deserve a good hiding from everyone.

A weasel hath not such a deal of spleen as you are toss'd with.

TRANSLATION: Not even a weasel is as loathsome as you.

Thou art a base, proud, shallow, beggarly, three-suited, hundred-pound, filthy, worsted-stocking knave; a lily-liver'd, action-taking knave; a whoreson, glass-gazing, superserviceable finical rogue; one-trunk-inheriting slave; one that wouldst be a bawd in way of good service, and art nothing but the composition of a knave, beggar, coward, pandar, and the son and heir of a mongrel bitch.

Your brain is as dry as the remainder biscuit after voyage.

TRANSLATION: There's not much going on upstairs with you.

He smells like a fish, a very ancient and fish-like smell.

TRANSLATION: He sure is a whiffy chap.

You have such a February face, so full of frost, of storm and cloudiness.

TRANSLATION: Lighten up you miserable wretch.

I do desire we may be better strangers.

TRANSLATION: I would dearly love to have nothing to do with you—starting now.

Peace, ye fat guts.

TRANSLATION: *Arrivederci*, porky!

Away you three-inch fool!

TRANSLATION:
Beat it, you little runt!

Sweep on, you fat
and greasy citizens!

TRANSLATION:
Get lost you odious creatures.

The devil a puritan that he is,
or anything constantly, but
a time-pleaser; an affectioned
ass that cons state without book
and utters it by great swarths.

TRANSLATION: He's nothing but a pompous
flatterer; a pretentious moron who thinks
way too much of himself.

*How low am I, thou
painted maypole?*

TRANSLATION: Well if I'm short, then you're
a lanky, make-up-smothered show-off.

No longer from head to foot
than from hip to hip, she is
spherical, like a globe, I could
find out countries in her.

TRANSLATION: She's really quite wide
(or possibly a Tudor "Yo mamma's
so fat...").

You scullion.
You rampallian.
You fustilarian.
I'll tickle your
catastrophe.

CHAPTER 5

19TH-CENTURY CHEAP SHOTS

19th-century Victorian English, Chinese, and French put-downs.

You were born under a threepenny halfpenny planet, never to be worth a groat.

TRANSLATION:
You worthless good for nothing.

You must be dicked in the nob walking round these parts, you cockalorum.

There's no need to be such a sneaksby.

Fàntǒng!

TRANSLATION:
You are an utterly useless person!
(Literally: you are a rice bucket!)

Fàng nǐ mā de gǒu chòu pì.

TRANSLATION:
What you said is bulls**t. (Literally: release
your mother's dog's stinky fart!)

Chaps, I appear to be chimping merry. I'm off with the jammiest bit of jam!

He looks like he'll shoot the cat before he visits the doodle sack...

TRANSLATION:
It's off to the cells with you, pimp!
And no more of the coarse language!

Here's a bunch of fives, you bracket-faced clodhopper!

TRANSLATION: This fist is for you, you ugly lout!

Kiss my cooler you chuckle-headed, cribbage-faced zounderkite!

TRANSLATION:
Kiss my ass you pock-marked, stupid idiot.

Lick-spittle!

URIAH HEEP & MR MICAWBER.

"David Copperfield."

You, sir, are a gentleman of four outs.

CHAPTER 6

WILD WEST WHIZZBANGERS

Cusses from cowboy country.

Jeez, your friend is as ugly as a burnt boot!

TRANSLATION:
Your associate is not
aesthetically pleasing.

Stop being a coffee boiler and go play the California prayer book with those spooney spoops!

But that sniptious whaler looks like a chiseler to me!

Listen skeezick. Put 'em up unless you want to be lying on your Sunday face in the dirt!

TRANSLATION:
Hey fathead. Put your hands up or else you'll be lying on your backside in the dirt!

How about I pour us some Kansas sheep dip and we talk? You'll see that someone is telling tarradiddles about me.

TRANSLATION:
Why don't we have some sippin' whiskey and a chat. I think you'll find that some guy is telling tall tales about me.

49

That fella in the corner sure is lushington. He's airing the lungs like nobody's business.

The chap in the corner is stinking drunk. He's swearing something rotten.

Looks like a barrel border to me.

Hey, I ain't no barrel border! I'm the biggest toad in the puddle in these parts!

He looks like a down-and-out to me.

I'm not a down-and-out (hiccup). I'm the top dog in this joint.

CHAPTER 7

20TH-CENTURY BURNS

Taunts from the turn of the century.

> *I had a flat tire with a canceled stamp last night...*

TRANSLATION:
I had a disastrous date with a bashful woman last night...

> *You can be as togged to the bricks as you like but you're still a face stretcher!*

> Stop casting a kitten. You're just upset because you were given the ice mitt last night.

You lousy gongoozler!

TRANSLATION: You bone-idle gawker!

I'd rather be a gongoozler than a spatherdab!

TRANSLATION:
Better that than a gossip-monger and a blabbermouth!

You're nothing but a schlemiel!

TRANSLATION: You're a clumsy loser!

Well at least I ain't no schmendrick!

TRANSLATION:
Yeah, well, you're a clueless mamma's boy!

You milky asterbar!

TRANSLATION:
You cowardly b**tard!

COCKNEY RHYMING SLANG

I fell on me bottle and glass when I was Brahms and Liszt.

TRANSLATION: I fell on my a**e (glass) when I was p**sed (Liszt = drunk).

That bloke's a right Hampton Wick.

TRANSLATION: That guy is a right p**ck (Wick).

I'm going to give that geezer a boot in the orchestras.

TRANSLATION: That chap (geezer) is going to get a kick (boot) in the balls (orchestra stalls).

You're a pain in the Khyber.

TRANSLATION: You're a pain in the a**e (Khyber Pass).

He's Patrick Swayze!

TRANSLATION: Steer clear, he's crazy (Swayze).

CHAPTER 8

CONTEMPORARY CURSES

Modern-day mockery.

Kisama tama!

(Japanese for "Lord of donkey balls.")

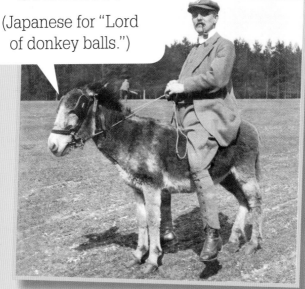

TRANSLATION:
I won't be writing you
a Christmas card this year.

Chipkali ke gaand ke pasine.

(Bengali for "Sweat of a lizard's ass.")

TRANSLATION:
You loathsome, foul-smelling creature.

Shattenparker!

(German for "A person who parks in the shade!")

TRANSLATION:
You insufferable wimp.

Sanjam da prdnem na tebe!

(Serbo-Croat for "I dream about farting on you.")

TRANSLATION:
I'm going to get you back SO badly.

Megi tröll hafa þína vini.

(Icelandic for "May the trolls take your friends.")

TRANSLATION:
I will not be hurrying out to purchase you a wedding gift.

PICTURE CREDITS

Front cover Getty Images/ De Agostini Picture Library.
Back cover Getty Images/Linda Steward. Page **2** Getty Images/
Universal History Archive; **6** Getty Images/National Galleries of
Scotland; **7** Getty Images/DEA PICTURE LIBRARY; **8** Getty Images/
Photo 12; **9** Getty Images/Universal Images Group; **10** Getty Images/
Universal History Archive; **11** Getty Images/Print Collector;
12 Getty Images/Culture Club; **13** Getty Images/Design Pics;
14 Getty Images/Hulton Archive/Handout; **15** Getty Images/SeM;
16 Getty Images/Universal History Archive; **18** Getty Images/Hulton
Archive/Handout; **19** Getty Images/Culture Club; **20** Getty Images/
Culture Club; **21** Getty Images/Hulton Archive/Stringer; **22** Getty
Images/Universal History Archive; **23** Getty Images/Print Collector;
24 Getty Images/Culture Club; **25** Getty Images/Print Collector;
26 Getty Images/De Agostini Picture Library; **28** Getty Images/
Culture Club; **29** Getty Images/Culture Club; **31** Getty Images/
Library of Congress; **32** Getty Images/Universal Images Group;
34 Getty Images/Archive Photos/Stringer; **35** Getty Images/Culture
Club; **36** Getty Images/Bildagentur-online; **37** Getty Images/Hulton
Deutsch; **38** Getty Images/Heritage Images; **39** Getty Images/
Universal History Archive; **40** Getty Images/Print Collector;
41 Getty Images/Print Collector; **42** Getty Images/Heritage Images;
43 Getty Images/Print Collector; **44** Getty Images/whitemay;
45 Getty Images/Culture Club; **46** Getty Images/Science & Society
Picture Library; **47** Getty Images/Culture Club; **48** Getty Images/
Bettmann; **49** Getty Images/MPI/Stringer; **50** Getty Images/
Fotosearch/Stringer; **51** Getty Images/Hulton Archive/Staff;
52 Getty Images/Historical Picture Archive; **53** Getty Images/
Print Collector; **54** Getty Images/DEA PICTURE LIBRARY; **55** Getty
Images/ullstein bild; **56** Getty Images/Hulton Archive/Stringer;
57 Getty Images/Bettmann; **59** Getty Images/Past Pix; **60** Getty
Images/Hulton Archive/Stringer; **61** Getty Images/Chris Hellier;
62 Getty Images/Universal History Archive; **63** Getty Images/
Culture Club